IVILIZATIONS OF THE WORLD

ANCIENT CHINA

by Samantha S. Bell

FOCUS READERS
NAVIGATOR

WWW.FOCUSREADERS.COM

Focus Readers is distributed by North Star Editions:
sales@northstareditions.com | 888-417-0195

Produced for Focus Readers by Red Line Editorial.

Content Consultant: Professor Pi-ching Hsu, Department of History, San Francisco State University

Photographs ©: Ke Wang/Shutterstock Images, cover, 1; Sirirat/Shutterstock Images, 4–5; Red Line Editorial, 7; bjdlzx/iStockphoto, 9; imaginechina/AP Images, 10–11; Jun Mu/Shutterstock Images, 13; Richie Chan/Shutterstock Images, 15; Vector Tradition/ Shutterstock Images, 16–17; dave stamboulis/Alamy, 19; Keren Su/China Span/Alamy, 21; Rudra Narayan Mitra/Shutterstock Images, 22–23; World Archive/Alamy, 25; Ian Dagnall/ Alamy, 27; loonger/iStockphoto, 29

Library of Congress Cataloging-in-Publication Data
Names: Bell, Samantha, author.
Title: Ancient China / by Samantha S. Bell.
Description: Lake Elmo, MN : Focus Readers, [2020] | Series: Civilizations of the world | Audience: Grades 4-6. | Includes bibliographical references and index.
Identifiers: LCCN 2019008550 (print) | LCCN 2019008943 (ebook) | ISBN 9781641859592 (pdf) | ISBN 9781641858908 (ebook) | ISBN 9781641857529 (hardcover) | ISBN 9781641858212 (pbk.)
Subjects: LCSH: China--Civilization--To 221 B.C.--Juvenile literature. | China--Civilization--221 B.C.-960 A.D.--Juvenile literature.
Classification: LCC DS741.65 (ebook) | LCC DS741.65 .B45 2020 (print) | DDC 931--dc23
LC record available at https://lccn.loc.gov/2019008550

Printed in the United States of America
Mankato, MN
May, 2019

ABOUT THE AUTHOR

Samantha S. Bell lives with her family in South Carolina. She graduated from Furman University with a degree in history and teaching certification in social studies. She is the author of more than 90 nonfiction books for children.

TABLE OF CONTENTS

CHAPTER 1

MANY DYNASTIES

Thousands of life-size statues form long rows. Clay soldiers hold weapons. Horses and chariots stand beside them. This underground army guards the tomb of Qin Shi Huang. He was the first ruler in China's Qin **dynasty**. But people had lived in China for thousands of years before he came to power.

The clay soldiers buried in Qin Shi Huang's tomb are known as the Terracotta Army.

Ancient writings tell of a Xia dynasty. They say it began around 2070 BCE. Some historians are not sure this dynasty existed. But **archaeologists** have found some evidence of it.

The Shang dynasty came next. It began around 1600 BCE. Historians have found many buildings and objects from this dynasty. The Shang built cities with palaces and temples. And they shaped bronze into containers and weapons.

Around 1050 BCE, a group of people called the Zhou rose up against the Shang ruler. They took control and started the Zhou dynasty. The Zhou began a belief called the Mandate of Heaven. It said only a **virtuous** person could rule. Heaven would cause a bad ruler to lose power.

The Zhou dynasty lasted 800 years. Gradually, its kingdom split into many states. The states fought one another.

DYNASTIES IN CHINA

By 221 BCE, a state called Qin had conquered the others around it. Its leader, Qin Shi Huang, became the first emperor of China. He also began the Qin dynasty. He led many building projects. New roads helped increase trade. And the Great Wall of China protected the land from attacks.

THE GREAT WALL

The Great Wall of China stretches for 4,000 miles (6,400 km). It is the longest human-made structure in the world. The wall began as separate **fortresses**. Most were built around 770 BCE. Qin Shi Huang connected the fortresses to form a wall. Over time, the wall began to fall apart. Later rulers rebuilt large parts of it. Much of their work can still be seen today.

The Great Wall of China was built and repaired over hundreds of years.

Qin Shi Huang died in 210 BCE. His son became the next emperor. But the people revolted. In 202 BCE, the Han dynasty took control. This family of rulers began many important traditions. Its leaders also set China on a path to become a world power.

CHAPTER 2

RULERS AND RELIGION

Kings ruled China during the Xia, Shang, and Zhou dynasties. Each king controlled an area known as a state. The king owned most of the land in this area. Many kings used a feudal system to rule their land. In this form of government, a king gave land to loyal followers. These followers became overlords.

Archaeologists have uncovered tombs from the Shang dynasty.

Each overlord ruled the people who lived on his land. The overlords sent soldiers to fight for the king.

This system changed when Qin Shi Huang united China. Qin emperors replaced the overlords with civil servants. These workers helped the emperor run

WRITING ON BONES

During the Shang dynasty, members of the royal court used oracle bones to tell the future. A **mystic** wrote the person's question on a bone or turtle shell. Then the bone or shell was heated. When it cracked, the mystic studied the crack to find the answer. Oracle bones show some of the earliest Chinese writing. Today, people read them to learn about ancient China.

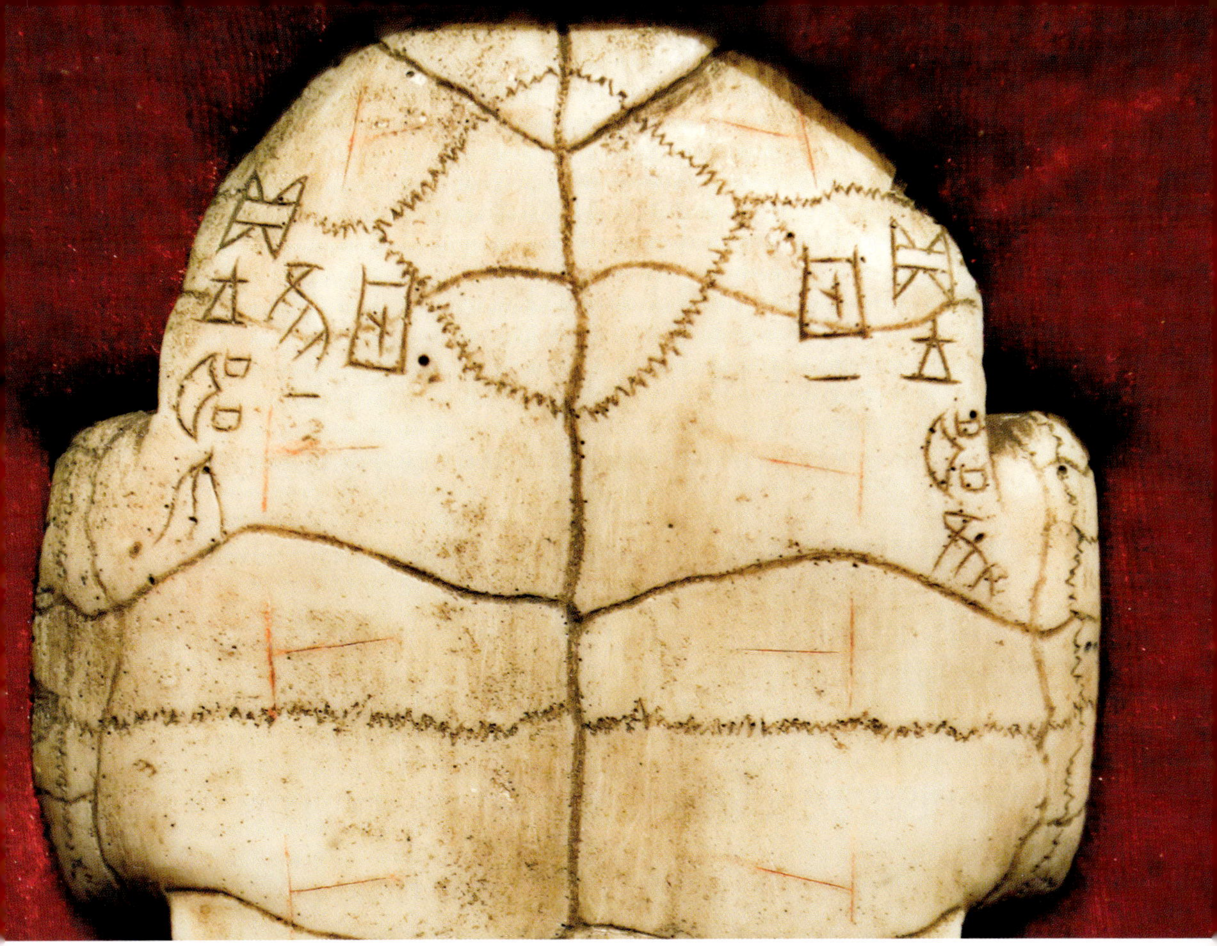

Oracle bones used during the Shang dynasty can be seen in some museums.

the government. They could become wealthy and powerful.

Religion in ancient China changed over time. During the Shang dynasty, people worshipped many gods and goddesses.

People also prayed and made offerings to the spirits of their **ancestors**. They asked these spirits for help and protection.

Many religious practices were based on **philosophy**. Taoism is one example. A man named Laozi created this philosophy around 500 BCE. He said a person's highest goal was to live at peace. His teachings included rules for how people should behave.

Confucianism began around the same time. It was started by Confucius. He lived from 551 to 479 BCE. Confucius developed rules for thinking and living a good life. He focused on self-discipline. Lots of people followed his teachings.

Part of practicing Confucianism involves visiting temples.

His ideas helped form standards for good behavior.

People often blended Buddhism with their other beliefs and practices. Buddhism began in India. But the religion spread to China during the Han dynasty. It taught that doing good would lead to lasting happiness.

CHAPTER 3

STRUCTURED SOCIETY

People in ancient China were divided by class. Showing respect to people of higher classes was very important. The emperor was at the top. Below him came four groups of people. Each group earned respect based on what its members did.

The *shi* came just below the emperor. At first, only warriors were in this class.

Dragons decorated the emperor's palace. They were symbols of power and authority.

Later, the *shi* class included scholars as well. The scholars studied how people should behave. They created many writings and laws.

Next came the *nong*. Members of this class were farmers. They owned land and grew crops. Because they provided food for everyone else, the *nong* were highly valued.

The *gong* class came after the *nong*. It included many types of artisans. These workers trained to make objects, such as porcelain, pottery, or silk. They were respected for their skills.

The lowest class was the *shang*. These people worked as traders and merchants.

The village of Xidi contains examples of what homes in ancient China looked like.

Some of them were wealthy. But they made nothing themselves. Instead, they bought and sold things other people had made. As a result, the *shang* earned less respect.

Respect played a key role in families, too. Men led the family. Children had to honor their fathers. Wives had to obey their husbands. Men also kept the family name going. So, people tended to value sons more than daughters.

WOMEN RULERS

Because men held a higher place in ancient China, most leaders were male. But there were a few exceptions. Lady Fu Hao was one of them. She married Wu Ding. He was a king in the Shang dynasty. Fu Hao became a general in his army. She won many battles. She also cast oracle bones. Another example was Wu Zetian. She ruled from 690 to 705 CE as China's only female emperor.

Paintings from ancient China often show scenes from nature or daily life.

People also valued art. Scholars wrote and painted to share their ideas. People believed the art showed their good character. Many scholars studied calligraphy, or the art of writing. They created symbols with a brush and ink. Each symbol represented a different word. Other artists used ink to paint pictures or worked with metal or clay.

CHAPTER 4

CHANGES IN CHINA

The Han dynasty lasted from 202 BCE to 220 CE. It was a time of great growth. China's **ethnic majority** became known as the Han Chinese. China built a huge **network** of trade routes called the Silk Road. The routes reached all the way to western Europe. They spread silk and spices throughout the ancient world.

Traders could travel along the Silk Road from China to western Europe.

After 220 CE, China entered a time of conflict. States and invaders fought for control. For years, China was divided into several kingdoms. The Sui dynasty, begun in 581 CE, finally united them in 589 CE.

This peace helped lead to the rise of the great Tang dynasty. The Tang ruled

A GREAT HISTORIAN

Sima Qian was one of China's earliest historians. He was born during the Han dynasty. His father, Sima Tan, started writing down the history of China. When Sima Tan died, Sima Qian continued his work. He spent the rest of his life finishing it. The book is called *Records of the Grand Historian.* It describes more than 2,000 years of China's history.

This painting shows people meeting Emperor Xuanzong.

China from 618 to 907 CE. Strong rulers brought peace and power. One emperor, Xuanzong, ruled for more than 40 years. Under him, China became the richest country in the world.

Fighting broke out again after the Tang fell. The Song restored order in 960 CE.

Once again, China began to grow. Cities and trade expanded during the Song dynasty. So did art and education.

By 1279 CE, however, the Mongols had invaded. Led by Kublai Khan, they began the Yuan dynasty. During this dynasty, art and trade stayed strong. But the Han Chinese faced **discrimination** from their foreign rulers.

The Ming dynasty took over in 1368 CE. Its rulers were Han Chinese. They helped spread China's influence around the world. Admiral Zheng He led one emperor's navy. His ships sailed throughout the Indian Ocean. They traveled as far as East Africa.

The Ming dynasty is famous for its porcelain, which is often decorated with blue designs.

China's last dynasty, the Qing, began in 1644 CE. Its rulers were Manchus, or people from the northeast part of China. A revolution in 1911 CE changed China's form of government. Emperors no longer ruled. But Chinese art and ideas still influence people around the world.

CREATING PAPER

During the Han dynasty, a Chinese man created the world's first paper. His name was Cai Lun. He was a servant of the emperor. At the time, people wrote on wooden tablets or slips of bamboo. Books were heavy and hard to carry.

Cai Lun wanted to find a better material. He tried using different types of plant fibers. First he soaked the fibers. Then he pressed them flat. When they dried, sheets of paper formed.

Around 105 CE, Cai Lun showed his process to the emperor. Papermaking spread quickly throughout China. At first, people mostly used the paper to wrap packages or make clothes. But by the Tang dynasty, people had started using it for writing.

Thanks to the Silk Road, paper spread to other countries. So did many other Chinese inventions.

Some people still practice traditional Chinese papermaking methods.

They include printing, gunpowder, and the compass. These ideas from ancient China are still used today.

FOCUS ON
ANCIENT CHINA

Write your answers on a separate piece of paper.

1. Write a paragraph describing one dynasty from China's history.

2. If you lived in ancient China, which art form would you most like to learn? Why would you choose that one?

3. Which class of people in ancient China was made up of farmers?

   A. the *gong*
   B. the *nong*
   C. the *shang*

4. How did Confucius influence life in ancient China?

   A. His teachings motivated people to make lots of changes.
   B. His teachings motivated people to respect and follow tradition.
   C. His teachings became the only official religion of China.

Answer key on page 32.

GLOSSARY

ancestors
Family members from the past.

archaeologists
People who study the ancient past, often by digging up buildings or objects from long ago.

discrimination
Unfair treatment based on people's looks or background.

dynasty
A series of rulers who all come from the same family.

ethnic majority
The group of people that make up the largest portion of an area's population.

fortresses
Large, strong buildings that can be defended from attack.

mystic
A person believed to have the ability to tell the future.

network
A large group of lines that cross or connect together.

philosophy
The study of truth, knowledge, and the meaning of life.

virtuous
Having good character qualities and doing good actions.

TO LEARN MORE

BOOKS

Atkins, Marcie Flinchum. *Ancient China*. Minneapolis: Abdo Publishing, 2015.

Kenney, Karen Latchana. *Mysteries of the Great Wall of China*. Minneapolis: Lerner Publications, 2018.

Spilsbury, Louise. *Ancient China*. Mankato, MN: Capstone Press, 2017.

NOTE TO EDUCATORS

Visit **www.focusreaders.com** to find lesson plans, activities, links, and other resources related to this title.

INDEX

Answer Key: 1. Answers will vary; **2.** Answers will vary; **3.** B; **4.** B